Quiz Book
For Seniors

-Multiple Choice Questions-

Whatever you choose to do, make sure you remember the golden rule...

Enjoy the Quiz

Table Of Content

1- What are the colors of the United States of America's flag?
A. Red, blue and green
B. Red, white and green
C. Red, white and blue
D. Red, blue and yellow

2- This sport consists of one player trying to throw a ball past another player who is trying to hit it. Which sport is it?
A. Soccer
B. Baseball
C. Football
D. Hockey

3- This fruit is typically eaten when it is yellow and one must peel it in order to get to the part that is edible. What fruit am I talking about?
A. Peach
B. Banana
C. Grape
D. Apple

4- Which of the following can typically be seen in the sky only at night time?
A. Sun
B. Clouds
C. Jet contrails
D. Shooting Stars

5- Which of the following countries is the smallest?
A. Canada
B. Italy
C. China
D. United States

Answer

1- Red, white and blue   2- Baseball
3- Banana
4- Shooting Stars   5- Italy

1- If Johnny mows one lawn a day and gets paid $10 to mow one lawn, how much money will he make in one week if he mows one lawn per day?

A. $50
B. $60
C. $70
D. $80

2- Which one of these dog breeds produces the largest dogs?

A. Great Dane
B. Poodle
C. Chihuahua
D. Dachshund

3- If one falls asleep at 10pm and wakes up at 8am, how many hours did this person sleep?

A. 9
B. 10
C. 11
D. 12

4- How many countries border Australia?

A. 0
B. 1
C. 2
D. 3

5- What hard structure protects the brain from injury?

A. Patella
B. Femur
C. Fibula
D. Skull

Answer

1- $70   2- Great Dane
3- 10   4- 0
5- Skull

.5.

1- What is the title of the United States of America's national anthem?
A. America the Beautiful
B. We Are The Champions
C. God Bless America
D. The Star Spangled Banner

2- If one were to visit the North Pole, which direction must one travel to get there?
A. South
B. North
C. East
D. West

3- If one is eating a burger, what kind of meat is the person most likely eating?
A. Beef
B. Badger
C. Penguin
D. Stork

4- If someone heard someone say the words Rose, Tulip and Marigold, what subject is the person most likely talking about?
A. Battleships
B. Cat breeds
C. Space shuttles
D. Flowers

5- In a typical deck of playing cards, which suits are red?
A. Spades and Clubs
B. Hearts and Diamonds
C. Diamonds and Clubs
D. Hearts and Spades

Answer

**1- The Star Spangled Banner   2- North
3- Beef   4- Flowers
5- Hearts and Diamonds**

1- Which of these is the fastest?
A. *Speed of light*
B. *Speed of sound*
C. *Speed of a jet*
D. *Speed of a snail*

2- Which one of the following website extensions is NOT a true website extension?
A. *.com*
B. *.edu*
C. *.org*
D. *.dot*

3- If you mix the colour red with the colour white, which colour will you end up with?
A. *Green*
B. *Purple*
C. *Pink*
D. *Beige*

4- Mixing blue and yellow paint together makes what color?
A. *Purple*
B. *Orange*
C. *Green*
D. *Red*

5- A figure with three sides is called a what?
A. *Pentagon*
B. *Triangle*
C. *Square*
D. *Octagon*

Answer

1- Speed of light   2- .dot
3- Pink   4- Green
5- Triangle

1- How long does it take the earth to revolve around the sun?
A. 365.2424 days
B. 1,440 minutes
C. 7 days
D. 24 hours

2- Which of these words is spelled incorrectly?
A. Necessity
B. Poliomyelitis
C. Empowerring
D. Discotheque

3- How long does it take for the moon to revolve around the earth?
A. About 1 week
B. About 2 weeks
C. About 1 month
D. About 1 year

4- What is the longest river in the world when NOT adding estuaries to the equation?
A. Zambezi
B. Nile
C. Mississippi
D. Amazon

5- Aviophobia is the fear of what?
A. Flying
B. Singing
C. Eating things with wings
D. Doctors

Answer
1- 365.2424 days   2- Empowerring (only one 'R')
3- About 1 month   4- Nile
5- Flying

1- Who was the first man to step on the moon?
A. Buzz Aldrin
B. John Glenn
C. Yuri Gagarin
D. Neil Armstrong

2- What is the capital city of the world's second smallest country by area?
A. Monaco
B. Funafuti
C. Vatican City
D. St. George's

3- Name the traditional and popular wrestling sport of Japan.
A. Kendo
B. Origami
C. Sumo
D. Ikebana

4- What number is represented by the letters XIX in Roman numerals?
A. 9
B. 19
C. 29
D. 29

5- Name the third known planet from the sun in our solar system.
A. Jupiter
B. Earth
C. Mars
D. Venus

Answer

1- Neil Armstrong 2- Monaco
3- Sumo 4- 19
5- Earth

1- What is the biggest living fish in the ocean?
A. Barracuda
B. Tuna
C. Whale Shark
D. Great white shark

2- How many months are there in the Muslim calendar?
A. 10
B. 12
C. 14
D. 16

3- Dracula suffers from staurophobia, the fear of _____?
A. Garlic
B. Mirrors
C. Daylight
D. Crucifixes

4- Which non-metallic element has the chemical symbol S?
A. Sulphur
B. Silicon
C. Sodium
D. Selenium

5- In which African country is Timbuktu?
A. Mali
B. Nigeria
C. Algeria
D. Chad

Answer

1- Whale Shark   2-12 (Hijiri calendar is a lunar calendar
3- Crucifixes   4- Sulphur
5- Mali

1- What year did Neil Armstrong land on the moon?
A. 1959
B. 1969
C. 1979
D. 1989

2- What is the 'basic unit of life'?
A. Cell
B. Organ
C. Molecule
D. Atom

3- Which of these colours is not on the flag of the Republic of Ireland?
A. Green
B. Red
C. White
D. Orange

4- Which of these is not a breed of dog?
A. Maltese
B. Great Dane
C. German Shepherd
D. Siamese

5- In what chain of restaurants could you buy a Big Mac?
A. McDonald's
B. Wendy's
C. Hungry Jack's
D. All of these

Answer
1- 1969   2- Cell
3- Red   4- Siamese (breed of cat)
5- McDonald's

1- In what board game can you build letter tiles up on top of one another to spell out words?

A. Upwords
B. Scrabble Jr
C. Monopoly
D. Scrabble

2- What is a Ponzi Scheme?

A. Landmark place in Japan
B. A new diet
C. Fraudulent investment scam
D. A design for a new Italian car

3- Who created the company Microsoft?

A. Steve Jobs
B. Walt Disney
C. Bill Clinton
D. Bill Gates

4- In the human body what are "sartorius", "biceps", "triceps" and "gluteus maximus"?

A. Veins
B. Teeth
C. Muscles
D. Bones

5- In which country is the city of Marrakesh located?

A. Egypt
B. Morocco
C. Turkey
D. Qatar

Answer

**1- Upwords 2- Fraudulent investment scam
3- Bill Gates 4- Muscles
5- Morocco**

1- Who or what is gumbo?
A. A soup or stew
B. Barnum and Bailey's first circus elephant
C. A person who has lost his or her dentures
D. A single Wellington boot

2- What is the official language spoken in Brazil?
A. Dutch
B. French
C. Portuguese
D. Spanish

3- Who became the longest-serving British monarch in 2015?
A. Henry III
B. Edward III
C. Elizabeth I
D. Elizabeth II

4- What area of science covers the study of living organisms?
A. Biology
B. Archeology
C. Physics
D. Chemistry

5- What word is French for "Thank you"?
A. Grazie
B. Merci
C. Spaciba
D. Gracias

Answer
1- A soup or stew   2- Portuguese
3- Elizabeth II   4- Biology
5- Merci

History

1- Which notorious man was born in Braunau am Inn, Austria on 20th April, 1889?

A. *Josef Stalin*
B. *Gustav Mahler*
C. *Adolf Hitler*
D. *Sigmund Freud*

2- Who was Genghis Khan?

A. *An actor who won an Oscar in 1933*
B. *The Mongol founder of the largest Eurasian empire in history*
C. *The Roman emperor who supported the persecution of monotheists*
D. *Egyptian pharaoh who was very extravagant*

3- Which of these countries has never been Communist?

A. *Vietnam*
B. *USSR*
C. *Cuba*
D. *Britain*

4- What one person is the swastika most associated with?

A. *Adolf Hitler*
B. *King George VIII*
C. *Alfred Mahan*
D. *Benito Mussolini*

5- What saying is widely attributed to Marie Antoinette in connection with the poor?

A. *Disband them!*
B. *Fetch them bread!*
C. *Let them eat cake*
D. *This is a sad day for France*

Answer

1- Adolf Hitler   2- "B"
3- Britain   4- Adolf Hitler
5- Let them eat cake

1- When did Christopher Columbus sail to America?

A. 1462
B. 1472
C. 1482
D. 1492

2- What was the ruler in ancient Egypt called?

A. Satrap
B. Durbar
C. Pharaoh
D. Sepoy

3- Which country, after seeking independence from the former Yugoslavia, brought the expression 'ethnic cleansing' into common usage?

A. Bosnia
B. Albania
C. Slovenia
D. Macedonia

4- Who was prime minister of the UK for most of the Second World War?

A. Winston Churchill
B. Randolph Churchill
C. Neville Chamberlain
D. Anthony Eden

5- Christopher Columbus' voyage to the Americas in 1492 opened up a new era in world history. What country sponsored his expedition?

A. Portugal
B. Spain
C. France
D. England

Answer

1- 1492   2- Pharaoh
3- Bosnia   4- Winston Churchill
5- Spain

1- Which structures were built in medieval times as a mixture of residence and defensive building?

A. Churches
B. Forts
C. Castles
D. Tombs

2- In which country in ancient times was mummification carried out on important people when they died?

A. Egypt
B. Greeks
C. Japan
D. India

3- Which people travelled in longships and raided Britain from Scandinavia in early medieval times?

A. Merovingian
B. Germanic kingdoms
C. Roman Empire
D. Vikings

4- With which queen is the phrase "We are not amused" connected?

A. Alexandra Feodorovna
B. Queen Elizabeth I
C. Queen Elizabeth II
D. Queen Victoria

5- Who was the first American President?

A. George Washington
B. Ronald Reagan
C. John Kennedy
D. Abraham Lincoln

Answer

1- Castles   2- Egypt
3- Vikings   4- Queen Victoria
5- George Washington

1- What was the name of the Frenchman who was a very clever soldier and helped his country win lots of battles?

A. Churchill

B. Napoleon

C. Hitler

D. Eisenhower

2- The telephone was first invented to help the deaf? but do you know who patented the design?

A. Alexander Graham Bell

B. Ronald Reagan

C. Sir Thomas Moore

D. Albert Einstein

3- Which country held the first Olympic Games?

A. Canada

B. Peru

C. Greece

D. Russia

4- Which European city was divided by a wall by which capitalism was to the west and Communism was to the east?

A. London

B. Paris

C. Madrid

D. Berlin

5- The Cold War was a war of words and hostility mainly between the USSR and which country?

A. Brazil

B. France

C. USA

D. Spain

Answer

1- Napoleon   2- Alexander Graham Bell

3- Greece   4- Berlin

5- USA

1- In 1969, three men were sent up into space in the Apollo missions. On what body in space did they land?

A: Mars
B: Venus
C: Sun
D: Moon

2- Tiananmen Square is a place in Asia that many view as the symbol of dictatorship and lack of free speech. In which country is Tiananmen Square?

A: India
B: Japan
C: China
D: Russia

3- Of what African country was Nelson Mandela the president?

A: South Africa
B: Libya
C: Zimbabwe
D: Egypt

4- What was the name of the Princess of Wales who unfortunately died in 1997 as a result of a car crash in Paris?

A: Anne
B: Mary
C: Margaret
D: Diana

5- On the 11th of September, 2001, New York City was hit by a tragedy. Many died in a terrorist attack on which of these buildings?

A. World Trade Center
B. CN Tower
C. Empire State Building
D. Sears Tower

Answer

1- Moon   2- China
3- South Africa   4- Diana
5- World Trade Center

1- In 2008, the 29th Olympic Games mainly took place in which Asian city
A. Tokyo
B. Sydney
C. Beijing
D. New Delhi

2- Which of these empires did the Huns, under Attila's leadership, battle with?
A. Mughal Empire
B. Roman Empire
C. Vijayanagara Empire
D. Brazilian Empire

3- Which U.S. president arranged the Lewis and Clark expedition, which was assisted by Sacagawea?
A. Woodrow Wilson
B. George Washington
C. Thomas Jefferson
D. Chester A. Arthur

4- Of the three ships used on Christopher Columbus' first voyage of exploration to the New World, which did not return to Spain?
A. Santa Maria
B. Pinta
C. Nina
D. They all returned

5- Which of these men is considered to be the first Roman emperor?
A: Plato
B: Marcus Aurelius
C: Augustus
D: Socrates

Answer

1- Beijing   2- Roman Empire
3- Thomas Jefferson   4- Santa Maria
5- Augustus

1- Which of these men was a famous Viking explorer?

A: Marco Polo
B: Sir Francis Drake
C: Leif Eriksson
D: Juan Ponce de Leon

2- In which country did Joan of Arc lead an army?

A: Switzerland
B: France
C: Germany
D: Poland

3- In which war was Benito Mussolini a leader and dictator?

A: Vietnam War
B: World War I
C: World War II
D: Trojan War

4- Which country did Britain start sending convicts to in the late 18th century?

A: Australia
B: USA
C: Canada
D: France

5- In Roman times, what did the townspeople have to pay to see a gladiator contest, or to watch a play?

A: A loaf of bread
B: A bottle of wine
C: More than a week's wages
D: Nothing, both were free

Answer

1- Leif Eriksson   2- France
3- World War II   4- Australia
5- Nothing, both were free

1- In what year did the Titanic sink?
A. 1910
B. 1912
C. 1914
D. 1916

2- What was the name of the bomb which was dropped on Hiroshima on 6 August 1945?
A. Blue Boy
B. Little Boy
C. Big Boy
D. Little Man

3- In what year did World War II start?
A. 1937
B. 1938
C. 1939
D. 1940

4- The Hundred Years War was fought between England and which other country?
A. France
B. Scotland
C. Italy
D. Germany

5- Which English queen was known as Gloriana?
A: Elizabeth I
B: Mary I
C: Anne
D: Victoria

Answer

1- 1912   2- Little Boy
3- 1939   4- France
5- Elizabeth I

1- Which lady made history when she became Prime Minister of Great Britain in 1979?
A. Betty Boothroyd
B. Bernadette Devlin
C. Margaret Thatcher
D. Nancy Astor

2- They had writers, mathematicians, sculptors, architects and philosophers who are admired today. Who were they?
A. The Etruscans
B. The Greeks
C. The Chinese
D. The Japanese

3- Their main city was in Italy but they conquered a large part of the world. They built the Colosseum, they built roads and aqueducts. Who were they?
A. The Egyptians
B. The Phoenicians
C. The Franks
D. The Romans

4- They were merchants and sailed in the Mediterranean. They learned how to dye fabric the color purple and had excellent vessels. Who were they?
A. The Phoenicians
B. The Mongols
C. The Persians
D. The Huns

5- It was the first civilization to use a written language and they go back 5000 years B.C. What are they collectively known as?
A: The Mesopotamians
B: The Minoans
C: The Huns
D: The Etruscans

Answer

1- Margaret Thatcher   2- The Greeks
3- The Romans   4- The Phoenicians
5- The Mesopotamians

1- This civilization built pyramids, used a writing system made of hieroglyphs, believed in inmortality. Who were they?

A. The Ethiopians
B. The Greeks
C. The Mongols
D. The Egyptians

2- This civilization goes back longer than any other one, they built the Great Wall to protect the country's borders. Who are they?

A. The Hittites
B. The Thebans
C. The Chinese
D. The Persians

3- They attacked cities on horseback, destroying and killing whoever was found on their paths. The most famous one of them was Attila. Who were they?

A. The Huns
B. The Celts
C. The Moors
D. The Franks

4- They were nomads who inhabited a large part of Central Asia and conquered more territory than any conqueror in the history of the world. Who were they?

A. The Vikings
B. The Mongols
C. The Goths
D. The Germans

5- This civilization lived in the north of Africa and invaded Spain in the 8th century, where they remained until 1492. Who were they?

A. The Moors
B. The Phoenicians
C. The Minoans
D. The Ethiopians

Answer

1- The Egyptians   2- The Chinese
3- The Huns   4- The Mongols
5- The Moors

1-True or false?
Napoleon Was Once Attacked By a Horde of Bunnies.
A. True
B. False

2- True or false?
Using Forks Used to Be Seen as Sacrilegious.
A. True
B. False

3- True or false?
There Were More Than 10 Plots to Kill Fidel Castro.
A. True
B. False

4- True or false?
Pope Gregory IV declared war on cats in the 13th Century.
A. True
B. False

5- True or false?
Ketchup Was Sold in the 1830s as Medicine.
A. True
B. False

Answer
1- True   2- True
3- False (600 Plots) 4- True
5- True

Geography

1- What mountain range runs along the western United States and is home to Pike's Peak?

A. The Rockies
B. The Himalayans
C. The Catskills
D. The Appalachans

2- What mountain is a very prominent geographic feature outside of Tokyo, Japan?

A. Mount Kilimanjaro
B. Mount Fuji
C. The Matterhorn
D. Mount Everest

3- Which of the following is not a body of water on Earth?

A. Arctic Ocean
B. Indian Ocean
C. The Sea of Tranquility
D. Pacific Ocean

4- What major body of water has historically been a huge point of contention in the Middle East, and separates Saudi Arabia from Iran?

A. The Dead Sea
B. The Suez Canal
C. The Tigris River
D. The Persian Gulf

5- The historic Alamo is in what U.S. state?

A: Arizona
B: Texas
C: New Mexico
D: Oklahoma

Answer

1- The Rockies   2- Mount Fuji
3- The Sea of Tranquility   4- The Persian Gulf
5- Texas

1- What is the world's largest hot desert? Hint -- it's in Africa?
A. The Sahara
B. The Kalahari
C. The Gobi
D. Antarctica

2-What area contains the lowest elevation in the United States?
A. Ocala National Forest
B. Llano Estacado
C. Death Valley
D. New Orleans

3- Which of the following is NOT one of the top five geographically largest countries in the world?
A. India
B. United States
C. Canada
D. Brazil

4- Which of the following countries does not border Afghanistan?
A. Pakistan
B. China
C. Iran
D. Russia

5- What major river in South America is home to the carnivorous pirahana?
A: Amazon
B: Rhine
C: Rio Grande
D: Nile

Answer

1- The Sahara   2- Death Valley
3- India   4- Russia
5- Amazon

1- What modern country is home to the ancient city of Babylon?
A. Jordan
B. Iran
C. Saudi Arabia
D. Iraq

2- This country, famous for tea, was once known as Ceylon. What is it called now?
A. India
B. Madagascar
C. Sri Lanka
D. Maldives

3- The Canadian city of York no longer exists. What is it called today?
A. Toronto
B. Ottawa
C. Hamilton
D. Vancouver

4- Many references in ancient history point to the Kingdom of Persia. What is the current name of this country?
A. Iran
B. United Arab Emirates
C. Saudi Arabia
D. Iraq

5- What is the only country to border both Venezuela and Paraguay?
A: Peru
B: Brazil
C: Colombia
D: Chile

Answer

1- Iraq   2- Sri Lanka
3- Toronto   4- Iran
5- Brazil

Which Country Am I Visiting?

1- Which country am I visiting if I am viewing the Eiffel Tower?
A. Spain
B. Brazil
C. France
D. Italy

2- Which country am I visiting if I am viewing the Leaning Tower of Pisa?
A. Japan
B. China
C. New Zealand
D. Italy

3- Which country am I visiting if I am viewing the Sydney Opera House?
A. Kenya
B. Australia
C. United States
D. Nigeria

4- Which country am I visiting if I am viewing the Lincoln Memorial?
A. United States
B. Thailand
C. Australia
D. India

5- Which country am I visiting if I am viewing the Canterbury Museum?
A: New Zealand
B: Haiti
C: Fiji
D: Jamaica

Answer
1- France   2- Italy
3- Australia   4- United States
5- New Zealand

Which Country Am I Visiting?

1- Which country am I visiting if I am viewing the Forbidden City?

A. Japan

B. Hong Kong

C. Korea

D. China

2- Which country am I visiting if I am viewing the Taj Mahal?

A. Swaziland

B. India

C. Russia

D. China

3- Which country am I visiting if I am viewing the Copenhagen Opera House?

A. Yemen

B. Cuba

C. Russia

D. Denmark

4- Afghanistan is a country in Central Asia that has borders with six others. Which is NOT one of them?

A. China

B. India

C. Pakistan

D. Iran

5- Which country am I visiting if I am viewing Osaka Castle?

A. Japan

B. Singapore

C. India

D. Poland

Answer

1- China   2- India

3- Denmark   4- India

5- Japan

1- In which country would you find Petra, a historical city famous for its beautiful rock carved structures?

A. Jordan
B. Peru
C. Egypt
D. China

2- What is the only country to border both Indonesia and Thailand?

A. Philippines
B. Myanmar
C. Singapore
D. Malaysia

3- Which nation plants more trees per person than any other country in the world?

A. Indonesia
B. Iceland
C. Ireland
D. Japan

4- What amazing natural feature would you be looking at if you were standing on the banks of the Niagara in the province of Ontario in Canada?

A. Waterfalls
B. Mammoth caves
C. Mountain range
D. Sand dunes

5- Which of the following countries is home to the El Castillo, a step pyramid found in the ancient Mayan city of Chichen Itza?

A: Norway
B: Mexico
C: Korea
D: Botswana

Answer

1- Jordan   2- Malaysia
3- Iceland   4- Waterfalls
5- Mexico

1- What nation, which borders 14 other countries, has the longest land borders of any country?

A. Ukraine
B. Mongolia
C. China
D. Turkey

2- Which of the following American cities is nicknamed the "Windy City"?

A. Washington
B. Los Angeles
C. New York
D. Chicago

3- Which Spanish city is associated with the event known as the 'Running of the Bulls'?

A. Seville
B. Pamplona
C. Barcelona
D. Madrid

4- Konnichi wa! Sushi is eaten along with other yummy foods like ramen and rice. What is this country called?

A. Mexico
B. Russia
C. China
D. Japan

5- Buon giorno! There are nice foods like spaghetti and pizza there. They used to use the lira as money. What is the country called?

A: Italy
B: Spain
C: France
D: Austria

Answer

1- China   2- Chicago
3- Pamplona   4- Japan
5- Italy

1- Where is Table Mountain?
A. Mozambique
B. South Africa
C. Tunisia
D. Zimbabwe

2- What is the currency of the Republic of Ireland?
A. Peso
B. Dollar
C. Euro
D. Pound Sterling

3- Which of the following is a city in Australia?
A. Adelaide
B. Chennai
C. Kuala Lumpur
D. Los Angeles

4- Which of these is an African country?
A. India
B. Malta
C. Mexico
D. Libya

5- What North American city hosted the 2002 Winter Olympics?
A: Los Angeles
B: Salt Lake City
C: New York
D: Washington DC

Answer
1- South Africa   2- Euro
3- Adelaide   4- Libya
5- Salt Lake City

1- Which of these is an Indian city?

A. Shanghai
B. Berlin
C. Kabul
D. New Delhi

2- In which country would you find pyramids and the Nile River?

A. South Africa
B. Egypt
C. Brazil
D. United States

3- To which country is the kangaroo native?

A. Chile
B. Morocco
C. Austria
D. Australia

4- In which country were fireworks invented?

A. China
B. U.K
C. Russia
D. United States

5- Where could you walk in the Black Forest and eat a delicious slice of Black Forest gateau?

A: Germany
B: Bulgaria
C: Portugal
D: Switzerland

Answer

1- New Delhi   2- Egypt
3- Australia   4- China
5- Germany

1- Which of the following countries is geographically NOT a part of Europe?

A. Ireland
B. Morocco
C. Iceland
D. Italy

2- Abraham Lincoln was a former president of which country?

A. United States
B. Mexico
C. Australia
D. France

3- In which country would you see the changing of the guard at Buckingham Palace?

A. Ireland
B. Scotland
C. Wales
D. England

4- Where would you be if you saw Big Ben, Stonehenge, and policemen called "bobbies"?

A. Canada
B. New Zealand
C. England
D. Germany

5- By what colourful nickname is Ireland sometimes known?

A: The Pearl Isle
B: The Emerald Isle
C: The Topaz Isle
D: The Ruby isle

Answer

1- Morocco 2- U.S.A
3- England 4- England
5- The Emerald Isle

1- Which continent is also a country when the word 'South' is added to it?

A. South America

B. Europe

C. Asia

D. Africa

2- In what large Asian country will you find the Yellow River?

A. China

B. Russia

C. Australia

D. Singapore

3- A river in South Africa, and a citrus fruit?

A. Lemon

B. Orange

C. Lime

D. Ugli

4- Island in the Mediterranean that gives its name to a small fish found mainly in tins?

A. Sardinia

B. Pilchardessos

C. Salmonela

D. Troute

5- Mountain range in California or a generic ingredient in candy?

A: Coffee

B: Chocolate

C: Caramel

D: Gum

Answer

1- Africa   2- China
3- Orange   4- Sardinia
5- Chocolate

Food
&
Drink

1- If you go to an Italian restaurant, which of these foods would you most likely find on the menu?
A. Stir-fry
B. Spaghetti
C. Burger
D. Burrito

2- Let's go to a Greek restaurant! What would you most likely find there?
A. Lamb
B. Pizza
C. Egg rolls
D. Burgers

3- Hola amigos! You are now visting a Mexican restaurant. What food would they most likely have?
A. Mashed potatoes
B. Chicken fingers
C. Pizza
D. Enchiladas

4- The next place you go to is a Japanese restaurant. What food is the most likely to be found on their menu?
A. Tacos
B. Sushi
C. Spaghetti
D. Burgers

5- An authentic American diner would most likely have which of the following foods?
A: Burgers
B: Stir-fry
C: Haggis
D: Burrito

Answer

1- Spaghetti 2- Lamb
3- Enchiladas 4- Sushi
5- Burgers

1- Egg rolls are most likely to be found at what type of restaurant?

A. Italian
B. French
C. American
D. Chinese

2- Which dessert is associated with Scotland?

A. Apple pie
B. Shortbread
C. Brownies
D. Carrot cake

3- Which bird is a common dish in France?

A. Duck
B. Flamingo
C. Ostrich
D. Penguin

4- Middle Eastern cuisine often uses what kind of bread?

A. Italian bread
B. Cinnamon swirl bread
C. Pita bread
D. Banana bread

5- Shellfish are most likely to be found in what type of cuisine?

A: Swiss
B: Caribbean
C: Mexican
D: German

Answer

1- Chinese 2- Shortbread
3- Duck 4- Pita bread
5- Caribbean

1- You are served a beautiful dish of lomi lomi salmon. Where is this most likely being offered to you?

A. Finland
B. Hawaii
C. Denmark
D. Colombia

2- A bonbon is any small candy or sweet which is coated with chocolate or fondant. From what country/language does the term derive?

A. France/French
B. Monaco/Monégasque
C. Germany/German
D. Holland/Dutch

3- According to the saying, what do you need to have one of a day to keep the doctor away?

A. Apple
B. Pear
C. Orange
D. Melon

4- Which of these should you eat or drink only little of to make sure you stay healthy?

A. Ice cream
B. Chocolate
C. Crisps
D. All of these

5- Satsumas and mandarins are both rich in vitamin C. What types of fruit are they?

A: Oranges
B: Nectarines
C: Apples
D: Grapefruit

Answer

1- Hawaii   2- France/French
3- Apple   4- All of these
5- Oranges

1- Which of these fruits are found mainly in Asia?
A. Mangosteen
B. Rambutan
C. Durian
D. All of these

2- What food can you get from most fast food restaurants, and is covered with lettuce, ketchup, and sometimes cheese?
A. Pancakes
B. Hot dog
C. Burger
D. Fried chicken

3- What food has meat, lettuce, tomatoes, and cheese wrapped in a corn tortilla shell?
A. Taco
B. Pizza
C. Burger
D. Kebab

4- What dessert has a dough outside with a fruit filling? "Sara Lee" is big in this industry.
A. Hot dog
B. Pie
C. Sourdough bread
D. Cake

5- When a chef juliennes a fruit or vegetable, the results look like which of the following?
A: Cubes
B: Crowns
C: Matchsticks
D: Coins

Answer

1- All of these   2- Burger
3- Taco   4- Pie
5- Matchsticks

1- What is the name given to the sweet, buttery pastry which often has a fruit, nut or plain iced (frosted) topping?

A. Danish pastry
B. Finnish pastry
C. Norwegian pastry
D. Swedish pastry

2- An American creation, the California roll is a variety of which Asian food?

A. Noodles
B. Bok choy
C. Bun cha
D. Sushi

3- In England, what is traditionally served with Yorkshire pudding?

A. Baked apples
B. Chicken and eggs
C. Roast beef
D. Baked salmon

4- When a recipe is described as 'Florentine', such as 'Eggs Florentine', 'Salmon Florentine' etc., which ingredient means 'Florentine'?

A. Carrot
B. Spinach
C. Garlic
D. Tomato

5- What is meant by the term 'Welsh rarebit'?

A: Cheese sauce on toast
B: Carrots in a cheese soufflé
C: Leeks baked with cheese
D: Rabbit pie with truffles

Answer

1- Danish pastry   2- Sushi
3- Roast beef   4- Spinach
5- Cheese sauce on toast

1- In which country would you find the following foods?
"Fish and chips, bangers and mash, steak and kidney pie, Eton mess"
A. Great Britain
B. Brazil
C. Korea
D. Pakistan

2- In which country would you find the following foods?
"Bratwurst, sauerkraut, schnitzel, pumpernickel bread"
A. Algeria
B. Germany
C. Argentina
D. Italy

3- In which country would you find the following foods?
"Vindaloo curry, chapatis, tandoori chicken, vegetable samosas"
A. Scotland
B. Iceland
C. Iraq
D. India

4- In which country would you find the following foods?
"Dim sum, chow mein, egg fried rice, Peking duck"
A. Spain
B. New Zealand
C. China
D. Turkey

5- In which country would you find the following foods?
" Pickled herring, meatballs, gravalax (cured salmon)"
A: Sweden
B: Hops
C: Fat
D: Malt

Answer

1- Great Britain   2- Germany
3- India 4- China
5- Sweden

1- Americans call them French fries. What do the British call them?

A. Skins
B. Crisps
C. Chips
D. Fries

2- What food are you most likely to find on your plate at a Chinese restaurant?

A. Steak
B. Pizza
C. Rice
D. Salad

3- Where in Europe would you have to travel if you wanted to try tapas and paella?

A. France
B. Greece
C. Italy
D. Spain

4- Fruit that is desiccated is prepared in what way?

A. Dried
B. Baked
C. Raw with a sugar glaze
D. Baked

5- Fettuccine, penne and lasagna are all kinds of what yummy food of Italian origin?

A: Bread
B: Pasta
C: Cake
D: Fish

Answer

1- Chips 2- Rice
3- Spain 4- Dried
5- Pasta

1- Which of these dishes is usually raw, and can also be Greek?

A. Omelet

B. Sasserole

C. Salad

D. Soup

2- Which of these is a spicy dish from India and Southeast Asia?

A. Curry

B. Candy

C. Celery

D. Cherry

3- What do the British reputedly like to drink every day at 5 o'clock?

A. Water

B. Juice

C. Coke

D. Tea

4- Frogs' legs are traditional to eat in which country?

A. Germany

B. France

C. Italy

D. Canada

5- What type of breakfast includes fried egg, sausages, baked beans, cooked tomato and toast with a cup of tea?

A: German Breakfast

B: Dutch Breakfast

C: English Breakfast

D: Australian Breakfast

Answer

1- Salad 2- Curry

3- Tea 4- France

5- English Breakfast

1- What flour is used in making one type of tortilla?
A. Teff flour
B. Rice flour
C. Tapioca flour
D. Corn flour

2- What type of chocolates are famous for their delicious taste?
A. Belgian Chocolates
B. Hungarian Chocolates
C. Swedish Chocolates
D. Indian Chocolates

3- Kung Pao Chicken is a dish from what country?
A. Bosnia
B. China
C. India
D. Japan

4- Biryani is a traditional dish from what country?
A. India
B. Sri Lanka
C. Bhutan
D. Malaysia

5- Pain au chocolat is a croissant filled with chocolate, but which country do they originate from?
A: Germany
B: Finland
C: France
D: Italy

Answer
1- Corn flour   2- Belgian Chocolates
3- China   4- India
5- France

1- Which of the following is not a type of oyster?
A. Damsons
B. Narennes
C. Colchester
D. Whitstables

2- In what country was the first commercial lemonade company documented?
A. Japan
B. China
C. England
D. France

3- What causes the blue veining in blue cheese?
A. Mold
B. Insects
C. A wrapper of mountain leaves
D. A special kind of milk

4- Which is not one of the elements in sugar?
A. Oxygen
B. Hydrogen
C. Carbon
D. Helium

5- Where is Darjeeling tea grown?
A: India
B: Egypt
C: China
D: Japan

Answer
1- Damsons   2- France (Compagnie de Limonadiers)
3- Mold   4- Helium
5- India

1- What ingredient gives American pumpernickel bread its dark color?
A. Bran
B. Wheat
C. Yeast
D. Molasses

2- If you served a fried alevin which of these would you be serving?
A. Fish
B. Lamb
C. Chicken
D. Veal

3- Which is not a type of mushroom?
A. Morel
B. Oyster
C. Bugouy
D. Cremini

4- What spice do chefs call the sweetwood?
A. Rosemary
B. Cinnamon
C. Sage
D. Oregano

5- Milanese style dishes are always prepared with what type of cheese?
A: Feta
B: Swiss
C: American
D: Parmesan

Answer

1- Molasses 2- Fish
3- Bugouy 4- Cinnamon
5- Parmesan

Animals

1- What is the smallest monkey in the world?
A. Lemur
B. Pygmy marmoset
C. Orangutang
D. Capuchin monkey

2- What rare bird can mimic any sound it hears, such as a chainsaw, a crying child, or a jackhammer?
A. Lyrebird
B. Parakeet
C. Macaw
D. Canary

3- What tiny, colorful bird flaps its wings at over 500 beats per minute?
A. Finch
B. Macaw
C. Hummingbird
D. Cockatiel

4- What animal lives on mountainsides and uses its horns for battle?
A. Moose
B. Elk
C. Mountain goat
D. Antelope

5- What bird lives in Antarctica, is often black and white in color and cannot fly?
A: Dodo
B: Penguin
C: Emu
D: Ostrich

Answer

1- Pygmy marmoset   2- Lyrebird
3- Hummingbird   4- Mountain goat
5- Penguin

1- What animal is golden brown in color, can grow to around six feet tall and carries its babies in its belly pouch?

A. Flying squirrel

B. Hyena

C. Kangaroo

D. Bush baby

2- What animal is small with a long tail, lives in sewers and carries disease deadly to humans?

A. Weasel

B. Black footed ferret

C. Rat

D. Cat

3- What animal has no legs, slides on its belly, can grow up to 600 pounds and can eat a pig whole?

A. Monocled cobra

B. Anaconda

C. Ball python

D. Garter snake

4- Which bird purrs or coos, is normally grey in color and is seen almost everywhere?

A. Puffin

B. Pigeon

C. Raven

D. Crow

5- What large cat is golden colored, the male has a big fuzzy mane and both male and female hunt other animals as food?

A: Bengal cat

B: Lion

C: House cat

D: Ferret

Answer

1- Kangaroo   2- Rat

3- Anaconda 4- Pigeon

5- Lion

1- Which of the following is not a kind of dog?
A. Basenji
B. Komondor
C. Dingo
D. Gnu

2- Which is not a recognised breed of cat?
A. Tortoiseshell
B. Rex
C. Siamese
D. Burmese

3- Which of the following fruits is a horse least likely to eat?
A. Apples
B. Pears
C. Oranges
D. Plums

4- Horses have four main paces. Which are these in order of speed? Put them slowest to fastest.
A. Walk, pace, gallop, trot
B. Walk, amble, trot, gallop
C. Pace, trot, walk, canter
D. Walk, trot, canter, gallop

5- How many teats do cows have?
A: Cows don't have teats. They have udders
B: Most of them have four, but a few have small extra ones
C: They always have four
D: They have two

Answer
1- Gnu 2- Tortoiseshell
3- Oranges 4- Walk, trot, canter, gallop
5- "B"

1- These colonizing insects might be kept in farms, and are sometimes uninvited guests at picnics. What insect is it?

A. Ants
B. Ladybugs
C. Mantis
D. Butterflies

2- These animals are closely related to humans, and they're practically family to Tarzan. Unlike monkeys, they do not have a tail. What animal is it?

A. Baboon
B. Duiker
C. Ape
D. Spider monkeys

3- This is a venomous snake, commonly believed to be used by Cleopatra to end her life. What animal is it?

A. Python
B. Asp
C. Cobra
D. Anaconda

4- While this could refer to a long feathery scarf worn around the neck, this animal is a non-venomous constrictor snake. What animal is it?

A. Boa
B. Titanoboa
C. Corn snake
D. Black mamba

5- This canine animal is often considered "man's best friend". What animal is it?

A: Dogs
B: Coyote
C: Wolf
D: Fox

Answer

1- Ants   2- Ape
3- Asp   4- Boa
5- Dogs

1- What "teddy bear" lives in eucalyptus trees and has strong, sharp claws and teeth that it will gladly use if scared and cornered?

A. Groundhog
B. Wolf
C. Koala
D. Drop bear

2- Ugly but cute in cartoon drawings, what hungry, hungry semiaquatic African mammal will attack and kill humans for no reason?

A. Hippopotamus
B. Lion
C. Dolphin
D. Zebra

3- It would rather stay hard at work in the water, but what busy, furry animal can slice through your arm with its cute buck teeth?

A. Snapping turtle
B. Mouse
C. Chipmunk
D. Beaver

4- What adorable, slow-moving, sad-eyed creature has venomous elbows?

A. Raccoon
B. Mongoose
C. Cobra
D. Slow loris

5- What tiny underwater creature looks like it's wearing four-legged, four-armed pajamas, but kills a few people a year with its bite?

A: Blue ringed octopus
B: Dolphin
C: Stingray
D: Piranha

Answer

1- Koala   2- Hippopotamus
3- Beaver   4- Slow loris
5- Blue ringed octopus

**1- It lives on tiny ants and termites,
but what silly looking creature can actually slash you open?**
A. Siberian tiger
B. American bullfrog
C. Yellow billed cuckoo
D. Giant anteater

**2- This human-size animal might seem fun to swim with,
until it drowns you. What Antarctic animal is it?**
A. Polar bear
B. Leopard seal
C. Bottlenose dolphin
D. Penguin

**3- What little fish has an adorable humanlike face,
but will likely poison you if you try to eat it?**
A. Clownfish
B. Shark
C. Eel
D. Pufferfish

**4- What critter might you see washing its "hands" in a stream?
You may recognize it more easily by the bandit mask on its face.**
A. Beaver
B. Raccoon
C. Skunk
D. Rat

**5- What flying mammal lives in a cave, eats mosquitoes
and hides during the day?**
A: Bat
B: Flying Fish
C: Flying Squirrel
D: Flying Lizard (Draco)

Answer

**1- Giant anteater   2- Leopard seal
3- Pufferfish   4- Raccoon
5- Bat**

1- Which of the following animals lives in a home called a formicary?

A. Raven

B. Warthog

C. Elephant

D. Ant

2- What is the common name for a beaver's home?

A. Burrow

B. Manor

C. Lodge

D. Castle

3- What animal would you find living in an aviary?

A. Okapi

B. Sparrow

C. Wolf

D. Cobra

4- Which of the following animals live in a home called a roost?

A. Cheetah

B. Worm

C. Giraffe

D. Bat

5- Which of the following animals would make its home in a structure called an eyrie?

A: Hawk

B: Koala

C: Gazelle

D: Rattlesnake

Answer

1- Ant   2- Lodge

3- Sparrow   4- Bat

5- Hawk

1- What is the first rule when you see an animal in the wild?
A. Kick the animal
B. Stroke the animal
C. Throw stones at the animal
D. Don't touch or go near the animal

2- Which of the following is the healthiest food to feed ducks in the park?
A. Sweets
B. Bird seed
C. Kellogg's cornflakes
D. Bread

3- What word describes stealing a wild animal without consent?
A. Boiling
B. Frying
C. Scrambling
D. Poaching

4- You have a pet cat. Which of the following does Kitty need every day?
A. Exercise
B. Fresh drinking water
C. Cat food
D. All of these

5- Which of these yummy foods should you never feed to a rabbit?
A: Lettuce
B: Cauliflower
C: Sultanas
D: Wholemeal bread

Answer

1- "D"   2- Bird seed
3- Poaching   4- All of these
5- Lettuce

1- Which domestic animal from Vietnam is very intelligent and can learn lots of tricks?

A. Miniature brahma
B. Goat
C. Ox
D. Pot Bellied Pig

2- Which beautiful birds from Africa are highly intelligent and can be taught many tricks and words?

A. Magpie
B. Hummingbird
C. Macaw
D. Grey Parrot

3- Which densely furred rodents from South America make good pets for older children and adults? They are very nice to stroke.

A. Ferrets
B. Pangolins
C. Norway Rats
D. Chinchillas

4- Which reptiles are known for their ability to camouflage themselves anywhere?

A. Chameleons
B. Alligators
C. Iguanas
D. Basilisks

5- Which animal is the largest rodent in the world and is from South America?

A: Porcupine
B: Capybara
C: Beaver
D: Woolly Rat

Answer

1- Pot Bellied Pig 2- Grey Parrot
3- Chinchillas 4- Chameleons
5- Capybara

1- The baby of a dolphin is called what?
A. A young
B. A dolphin
C. Baby dolphin
D. Calf

2- The biggest animal in the world is a kind of whale. What is the biggest whale?
A. The Prince of Wales
B. The Blue Whale
C. The Dolphin
D. The Beluga

3- What is the biggest kind of fish?
A. The Guppy
B. The Whale Shark
C. The Sea Horse
D. The Tuna Salad Sandwich

4- What is the biggest cat?
A. The Burmese
B. Top Cat
C. The Siberian Tiger
D. The Lynx

5- What is the largest bear?
A: A Boy Dressed as a Bear
B: The Kodiak Bear
C: The Sun Bear
D: Yogi Bear

Answer
1- Calf   2- The Blue Whale
3- The Whale Shark   4- The Siberian Tiger
5- The Kodiak Bear

1- It's the largest bird in the world. What kind of bird is it?
A. Duck duck
B. Goose
C. Ostrich
D. Humming bird

2- What is the largest (heaviest) land animal?
A. The Poodle
B. Bugs Bunny
C. The Mouse
D. The Elephant

3- What is the tallest animal on land?
A. The Anteater
B. The Okapi
C. The Giraffe
D. The Squirrel

4- What are fruit bats also known as?
A. Flying mouse
B. Flying rat
C. Flying fox
D. Flying squirrel

5- Why do some snakes pretend to be dead?
A. To escape from enemies
B. For fun
C. To catch their food
D. They don't - they are dead

Answer

1- Ostrich   2- The Elephant
3- The Giraffe   4- Flying fox
5- To escape from enemies

World Capitals

1- The capital city of New Zealand is considered the windiest city in the world. Which city is this?

A. Queenstown
B. Wellington
C. Auckland
D. Dunedin

2- What is the capital of the windiest country in the United Kingdom?

A. Belfast
B. Edinburgh
C. London
D. Cardiff

3- Canada's capital, known for its beautiful canal.

A. Montreal
B. Toronto
C. Ottawa
D. Ontario

4- The capital of the USA, known for its grand monuments.

A. Chicago
B. New York
C. Washington, D.C.
D. Pennsylvania

5- The capital of Australia, a small park-like city.

A: Brisbane
B: Melbourne
C: Canberra
D: Sydney

Answer

1- Wellington   2- Edinburgh
3- Ottawa   4- Washington, D.C.
5- Canberra

1- The capital of the UK, known for its famous river.

A. Belfast
B. Swansea
C. Dublin
D. London

2- The capital of Sweden, sometimes called "The Venice of the North".

A. Copenhagen
B. Stockholm
C. Helsinki
D. Oslo

3- The capital of Peru, founded by Francisco Pizarro.

A. La Paz
B. Georgetown
C. Lima
D. Bogota

4- The capital of Denmark, known for its Tivoli Gardens.

A. Odense
B. Copenhagen
C. Helsinki
D. Oslo

5- The capital of Switzerland, the fifth most populous in the country.

A. Bern
B. Zürich
C. Geneva
D. Vienna

Answer

1- London   2- Stockholm
3- Lima   4- Copenhagen
5- Bern

1- The capital of Finland, known for its beautiful scenery.
A. Porvoo
B. Mikkeli
C. Helsinki
D. Imatra

2- The capital of Germany, known for the wall that is no longer there.
A. Hamburg
B. Berlin
C. Paris
D. Budapest

3- Located on Kaafu Atoll, of what country is Malé the capital?
A. Malta
B. Maldives
C. Chad
D. Jamaica

4- In which capital city could you find monuments like
the Louvre Museum, Notre Dame and most famously, the Eiffel tower?
A. Paris
B. Madrid
C. Berlin
D. Bordeaux

5- What is the capital of the country whose population
reached 1 billion in 1999?
A. Shanghai
B. Kolkata
C. Beijing
D. New Delhi

Answer

1- Helsinki   2- Berlin
3- Maldives   4- Paris
5- New Delhi

1- What is the legislative capital of South Africa?
A. Cape Town
B. London
C. Bloemfontein
D. Pretoria

2- What Asian capital is near the confluence of the rivers Baghmati and Vishnumati?
A. New Delhi, India
B. Beijing, China
C. Dakar, Senegal
D. Kathmandu, Nepal

3- Which capital city is situated on the slopes of the Pichincha volcano?
A. Porto Novo, Benin
B. Quito, Ecuador
C. Mexico City, Mexico
D. Madrid, Spain

4- In which capital city is Red Square?
A. Moscow
B. St. Petersburg
C. Warsaw
D. Tblisi

5- Bangladesh is one of the poorest countries in the world. What is the country's largest and most populous city?
A. Mumbai
B. Dhaka
C. Kolkata
D. Islamabad

Answer

1- Cape Town   2- Kathmandu, Nepal
3- Quito, Ecuador   4- Moscow
5- Dhaka

1- Name the Egyptian capital city that lies along the longest river in the world.

A. San Marino
B. Tripoli
C. Cairo
D. Giza

2- Sierra Leone is one the poorest places in the world. Guess the name of its largest city, which is also its capital.

A. Freetown
B. Bumbuna
C. Port Loko
D. Sierra Town

3- Indonesia is made up of 17,508 islands. Which capital city, found in Java, was once called Batavia?

A. Ja
B. Jakarta
C. Bangkok
D. Kuala Lumpur

4- Argentina's capital city's name means "good air" or "favourable winds" and is home to the famous Botanical Gardens.

A. Buenos Aires
B. Bogota
C. Santiago
D. Lima

5- Uzbekistan is the 55th largest country in the world. What capital city is well-known for its beautiful parks and mosques?

A. Dili
B. Beijing
C. Tashkent
D. Thimphu

Answer

1- Cairo   2- Freetown
3- Jakarta   4- Buenos Aires
5- Tashkent

1- Nouakchott is the capital of?

A. Djibouti
B. Eritrea
C. Mauritania
D. Cape Verde

2- Harare is the capital of?

A. Zimbabwe
B. Kenya
C. Zambia
D. Tanzania

3- Niamey is the capital of?

A. Nigeria
B. Namibia
C. Mauritania
D. Niger

4- Libreville is the capital of?

A. Gambia
B. Lesotho
C. Gabon
D. Guinea

5- Antananarivo is the capital of?

A. Mauritania
B. Madagascar
C. Mozambique
D. Mauritius

Answer

1- Mauritania   2- Zimbabwe
3- Niger 4- Gabon
5- Madagascar

1- Situated in a central valley, where is the capital city of Santiago located?

A. *Argentina*

B. *Bolivia*

C. *Chile*

D. *Brazil*

2- Havana, a port city and capital, is found in which country?

A. *Antigua and Barbuda*

B. *Cuba*

C. *Bahamas*

D. *Jamaica*

3- The capital city Nuuk is the largest and most populous city of which autonomous region?

A. *Scotland*

B. *Norway*

C. *Iceland*

D. *Greenland*

4- Vaduz is the capital city and seat of parliament for which country?

A. *Liechtenstein*

B. *Austria*

C. *Switzerland*

D. *Czech Republic*

5- Spain's capital city is found along the Manzanares River. Name it.

A. *Madrid*

B. *Sevilla*

C. *Barcelona*

D. *Valencia*

Answer

1- Chile   2- Cuba

3- Greenland   4- Liechtenstein

5- Madrid

1- Kingston is the capital of?
A. Haiti
B. Jamaica
C. St. Vincent and Grenadines
D. Dominican Republic

2- George Town is the capital of?
A. British Virgin Islands
B. Turks and Caicos Islands
C. Cayman Islands
D. Virgin Islands (USA)

3- Hamilton is the capital of?
A. Bermuda
B. Barbuda
C. Bonaire
D. Bahamas

4- Which city is located at the River Liffey's mouth, and is Ireland's capital?
A. Kerry
B. Dublin
C. Shannon
D. Cork

5- What is the administrative capital of Sri Lanka?
A. Moratuwa
B. Negombo
C. Colombo
D. Sri Jayawardenapura-Kotte

Answer

1- Jamaica   2- Cayman Islands
3- Bermuda 4- Dublin
5- Sri Jayawardenapura-Kotte

1- Which city became the capital of the Philippines in 1976?
A. Tokyo
B. Manila
C. New Delhi
D. Santa Cruz

2- Which Icelandic city is the country's center of government and is known for its geologically active volcanoes?
A. Reykjavik
B. Akureyri
C. Borgarnes
D. Selfoss

3- What is the capital of Somalia?
A. Jilib
B. Eyl
C. Badhan
D. Mogadishu

4- What is the capital of Romania?
A. Timisoara
B. Bucharest
C. Iasi
D. Galati

5- What is the capital of Greece?
A. Piraeus
B. Patras
C. Athens
D. Thessaloniki

Answer
1- Manila   2- Reykjavik
3- Mogadishu   4- Bucharest
5- Athens

1- True or false?
South Africa is home to the most national capital cities in the world.

A. True
B. False

2- True or false?
Wellington, New Zealand, is the southernmost capital in the world.

A. True
B. False

3- True or false?
La Paz in Bolivia is the highest capital city in the world.

A. True
B. False

4- True or false?
Reykjavik in Iceland is the most northerly capital in the world.

A. True
B. False

5- True or false?
Tokyo (Japan) is also known for being the most "natural disaster-prone" city in the world.

A. True
B. False

Answer

1- True (Cape Town, Pretoria, and Bloemfontein)
2- True   3- True   4- True
5- True

1- True or false?
Ottawa, Canada is the seventh coldest capital city in the world.
A. True
B. False

2- True or false?
Lima, Peru is the third most populous desert city.
A. True
B. False

3- True or false?
Georgetown is the capital city of Ascension Island and doesn't have a school.
A. True
B. False

4- True or false?
Casablanca, Morocco is largest city in Africa.
A. True
B. False

5- True or false?
Malabo in Equatorial Guinea is the only capital city in Africa where Spanish is the official language.
A. True
B. False

Answer
1- True   2- True
3- True   4- False (Cairo, Egypt)
5- True

Sports

American Football:

1- Which player on the football team usually throws the football?

A. Tackle
B. Quarterback
C. Wide Receiver
D. Running Backs

2- Who usually catches the ball on a football team?

A. Wide Receiver
B. Quarterback
C. Punter
D. Guard

3- Who usually runs with the ball?

A. Kicker
B. Safety
C. Running Back
D. Center

4- Which one of these words means to knock a person down in footballs?

A. Fumble
B. Interception
C. Tackle
D. Punt

5- How many points does a team get for a touchdown in American football?

A. 4
B. 5
C. 6
D. 7

Answer

1- Quarterback   2- Wide Receiver
3- Running Back 4- Tackle
5- 6

Soccer / Football:

1- Which is the club where Argentinian player Diego Armando Maradona became an idol?

A. River Plate
B. Sampdoria
C. Napoli
D. Real Madrid

2- Gabriel Batistuta is a native of which South American Country?

A. Argentina
B. Paraguay
C. Brazil
D. Chile

3- Who played his first game for Argentina in 2005, when he was 18 years old, wearing the number 10 jersey?

A. Wayne Rooney
B. David Villa
C. Lionel Messi
D. Cristiano Ronaldo

4- This Brazilian won the World Cup three times, and he is considered by many to be the best player of all time. Who is he?

A. Ronaldinho
B. Socrates
C. Romario
D. Pelé

5- Which player was awarded the Order of Lenin by the Soviet government in 1968?

A. Fernc Puskas
B. Victo Onopko
C. Alexander Blokhin
D. Lev Yashin

Answer

1- Napoli   2- Argentina
3- Lionel Messi
4- Pelé   5- Lev Yashin

Soccer / Football:

- What's the first name of Zidane the former French international player?

A. Zinedine
B. Zizu
C. Zinezine
D. Zizou

2- What's the first name of the former Manchester United player Beckham?

A. John
B. Robbie
C. Paul
D. David

3- When was the first FIFA World Cup played?

A. 1926
B. 1930
C. 1934
D. 1938

4- Where was the first FIFA World Cup played?

A. Italy
B. Germany
C. Brazil
D. Uruguay

5- Who won the first FIFA World Cup?

A. Uruguay
B. Brazil
C. Germany
D. Argentina

Answer

1- Zinedine   2- David
3- 1930   4- Uruguay
5- Uruguay

Basketball / NBA:

1- What does NBA stand for?
A. National Basketball Alliance
B. Nationwide Basketball Athleticism
C. National Basketball Association
D. No Basketball Allowed

2- Which Chinese born player became a member of the Houston Rockets in the 2002-03 season?
A. Lauren Woods
B. Tim Duncan
C. Yao Ming
D. Shaquile O'Neal

3- How long is a regular NBA ball game?
A. 46 minutes
B. 48 minutes
C. 50 minutes
D. 52 minutes

4- Who first invented basketball?
A. John Wooden
B. James Naismith
C. William G. Morgan
D. Phog Allen

5- Who was the first player to score 100 Points in a game?
A. Wilt Chamberlain
B. Michael Jordan
C. Larry Bird
D. Oscar Robertson

Answer
1- "C" 2- Yao Ming
3- 48 minutes 4- James Naismith
5- Wilt Chamberlain

Basketball / NBA:

- What coach won 8 straight championships with the Boston Celtics?

A. Bill Russell

B. Red Auerbach

C. Phil Jackson

D. John Havlicek

2- Who won the first NBA championship ever in the year of 1947?

A. Philadelphia Warriors

B. Kansas City Kings

C. Chicago Stags

D. Minneapolis Lakers

3- Who played the most NBA seasons in history?

A. Karl Malone

B. Michael Jordan

C. Vince Carter

D. Dirk Nowitzki

4- Who has the most assists in NBA history?

A. Jason Kidd

B. Mark Jackson

C. CHRIS PAUL

D. John Stockton

5- Who has the record for most 3-Pointers in a single game?

A. Zach LaVine

B. Ray Allen

C. Stephen Curry

D. Klay Thompson

Answer

1- Red Auerbach   2- Philadelphia Warriors
3- Vince Carter   4- John Stockton
5- Klay Thompson

Baseball / MLB:

1- What is the dirt area between the outfield grass and the home run wall called?

A. Warning track
B. Coaching box
C. Bullpen
D. Warning track

2- What do players call the area where relief pitchers practice before playing a game?

A. Bullpen
B. Crib
C. Cage
D. Stall

3- Where is the National Baseball Hall of Fame and Museum located?

A. St. Louis, Missouri
B. Scranton, Pennsylvania
C. Cooperstown, New York
D. San Diego, California

4- What word is used to describe a left-handed pitcher?

A. Left-hander
B. Leftie
C. Northpaw
D. Southpaw

5- Which Major League baseball player was known as the 'Bambino'?

A. Babe Ruth
B. Abraham Lincoln
C. Pac-Man
D. Bambi Orwell

Answer

1- Warning track   2- Bullpen
3- Cooperstown, New York   4- Southpaw
5- Babe Ruth

Baseball / MLB:

1- Which one of these ways is a fielder not allowed to catch the ball?

A. With his mitt

B. With his cap

C. With his bare hands

D. None of these

2- How many bases are there in a baseball infield?

A. 2

B. 4

C. 6

D. 8

3- The first World Series occurred in which year?

A. 1903

B. 1923

C. 1943

D. 1963

4- In which year was the spitball banned from baseball?

A. 1920

B. 1930

C. 1940

D. 1950

5- Who was the first baseballer to play in 3000 games?

A. Cy Young

B. Ty Cobb

C. Phil Niekro

D. Rollie Fingers

Answer

1- With his cap   2- 4

3- 1903   4- 1920

5- Ty Cobb

Boxing:

1-Muhammad Ali KO's Sonny Liston in the seventh round, won the title for him in which year?

A. 1964

B. 1974

C. 1984

D. 1994

2- Mike Tyson became the youngest heavyweight champion with a second round KO over which boxer in 1986?

A. James "Bonecrusher" Smith

B. Trevor Berbick

C. Pinklon Thomas

D. Mitch Green

3- In 1997, whose ear was gouged by a bite from Mike Tyson?

A. Razor Ruddock

B. Tony Tucker

C. Jack Dempsey

D. Evander Holyfield

4- What was heavyweight champ Muhammad Ali's birth name?

A. Jack Sharkey

B. Cassius Clay

C. Tony Tubbs

D. Rodriguez Marsh

5- At 49-0, who was the only undefeated heavyweight of the 20th century?

A. Rocky Marciano

B. Jack Dempsey

C. Jim Corbett

D. Joe Louis

Answer

1- 1964   2- Trevor Berbick

3- Evander Holyfield   4- Cassius Clay

5- Rocky Marciano

Boxing:

1- Who broke Muhammad Ali's jaw in 1973, during their first fight?
A. Joe Frazier
B. Ken Norton
C. Sonny Liston
D. George Foreman

2- When Muhummad Ali's title was revoked by the WBA in 1967 for refusing the draft during the Vietnam War, who inherited the title?
A. Floyd Patterson
B. Ken Norton
C. George Foreman
D. Jimmy Ellis

3- Who is the only fighter to win three consecutive Olympic medals in the same weight class?
A. Muhummad Ali
B. Julio Cesar Chavez
C. Sugar Ray Robinson
D. Teofilo Stevenson

4- Junior welterweight champ Frankie Randall had what nickname?
A. Iron Fist
B. The Dictator
C. The Surgeon
D. Razor

5- Whose nickname was "The Louisville Lip"?
A. James Pritchard
B. Muhammad Ali
C. Greg Page
D. Jimmy Ellis

Answer

1- Ken Norton   2- Jimmy Ellis
3- Teofilo Stevenson   4- The Surgeon
5- Muhammad Ali

The Olympics:

1- The first Olympic games in Greece were held how often?

A. Every year

B. Every two years

C. Every four years

D. Every six years

2- What colors are the Olympic rings?

A. Blue, maroon, purple, green and red

B. Blue, maroon, black, green and red

C. Blue, yellow, black, green and red

D. Blue, yellow, black, green and Pink

3- Which country has hosted the most Olympic Games?

A. United States

B. United Kingdom

C. China

D. Japan

4- Which city has hosted the Olympics three times?

A. New York

B. Paris

C. London

D. Beijing

5- The 1940 Olympic relay was never completed. For what reason?

A. Heavy rainfall waterlogged the Cauldron

B. Someone dropped the torch

C. Wind blew out the Flame

D. The Games were canceled

Answer

1- Every four years   2- "C"

3- United States   4- London

5- The Games were canceled

The Olympics:

1- Which American Olympic athlete was later a prisoner of war in World War II?

A. Jack O'Connell

B. Mutsuhiro Watanabe

C. Louis Zamperini

D. Pete Zamperini

2- What year did the NBA "Dream Team" participate in the Olympics?

A. 1988

B. 1992

C. 1996

D. 2000

3- Which male gymnast won four gold medals in a single day?

A. Alexei Nemov

B. Vitaly Scherbo

C. Boris Shakhlin

D. Li Xiaoshuang

4- The Olympics were suspended for 36 hours after a terrorist attack in which city's Olympic Village?

A. Munich

B. London

C. Moscow

D. Beijing

5- Who was the first Olympic athlete to be disqualified for testing positive for steroids?

A. Marion Jones

B. Donovan Bailey

C. Linford Christie

D. Ben Johnson

Answer

1- Louis Zamperini 2- 1992
3- Vitaly Scherbo 4- Munich
5- Ben Johnson

Science

1- What is the chemical formula for water?

A. HO_2

B. H_2O

C. H_2O_2

D. H_3O

2- What does a caterpillar change into?

A. Frog

B. Beetle

C. Butterfly

D. Spider

3- What are clouds made of?

A. Gas

B. Cotton wool

C. White sand

D. Water

4- How many colours are there in a rainbow?

A. 5

B. 6

C. 7

D. 8

5- If an animal is a carnivore, what does it do?

A. It eat plants

B. It eats meat

C. It eat both plants and meat

D. None of these

Answer

1- H_2O 2- Butterfly

3- Water   4- 7

5- It eats meat

1- What is the name of the force that holds everything to the earth?

A. Air

B. Gravity

C. Power

D. Entropy

2- Which of the following travels the fastest?

A. Airplane

B. Car

C. Sound

D. Light

3- What do you call a scientist who studies the stars?

A. Astronomer

B. Biologist

C. Chemist

D. Geologist

4- What is the name of this line that splits the Earth in half and is the hottest place on Earth?

A. The Equator

B. The Tropic of Cancer

C. The Tropic of Capricorn

D. The Arctic Circle

5- What is the name of the organ in our bodies that pumps blood?

A. Lungs

B. Heart

C. Brain

D. Liver

Answer

1- Gravity 2- Light

3- Astronomer 4- The Equator

5- Heart

1- What is the name of the gas in the air that keeps us alive?

A. Oxygen

B. Argon

C. Carbon dioxide

D. Nitrogen

2- Which of these living things does NOT have a backbone?

A. Human

B. Dog

C. Earthworm

D. Cat

3- If I dissolve some sugar in water, what have I made?

A. A solvent

B. A solution

C. A solute

D. A cup of tea

4- Planet Earth is the _____ planet from the Sun.

A. Second

B. Third

C. Fifth

D. Seventh

5- What do we call the natural process by which the weather and the sea wear away the land?

A. Exposure

B. Erosion

C. Vulcanism

D. Precipitation

Answer

1- Oxygen   2- Earthworm
3- A solution   4- Third
5- Erosion

1- What is the two digit numeric system, that only uses 0 and 1, that computers operate using?

A. Python
B. Binary
C. Java
D. JavaScript

2- What does "WWW" stand for?

A. World War Web
B. World Wide Wifi
C. World Wide Web
D. World Wifi Web

3- Who developed the first web browser?

A. Jimmy Wales
B. Robert Cailliau
C. Larry Page
D. Tim Berners-Lee

4- Name the layer which protects our earth from harmful rays?

A. Ozone
B. Water
C. Cloud
D. Methane

5- What is the nearest planet to the Sun?

A. Mars
B. Mercury
C. Venus
D. Jupiter

Answer

1- Binary   2- World Wide Web
3- Tim Berners-Lee   4- Ozone
5- Mercury

1- How many bones are there in a human body?
A. 106
B. 156
C. 206
D. 256

2- How many teeth an adult human has?
A. 28
B. 32
C. 36
D. 40

3- How much is percent water present on the earth?
A. 41%
B. 51%
C. 61%
D. 71%

4- Name the largest planet in the solar system.
A. Jupiter
B. Earth
C. Mars
D. Venus

5- What is the other name Deuterium?
A. Light water
B. Heavy water
C. Water
D. Steam

Answer

1- 206   2- 32
3- 71%   4- Jupiter
5- Heavy water

1- How many components made up the human blood?

A. 2

B. 3

C. 4

D. 5

2- Name the person who studies animals?

A. Psychologist

B. Zoologists

C. Anthropologist

D. Biologist

3- Which pigment determines the color of the human skin?

A. Protein

B. Platelets

C. Plasma

D. Melanin

4- Who was the first person to name cells cells?
"The person who discovered Human cell."

A. Edward Jenner

B. Robert Hooke

C. Theodor Schwann

D. Isaac Newton

5- Which side of brain controls the left side of the human body?

A. Left & Right side

B. Left side

C. Right side

D. None of These

Answer

1- 4   2- Zoologists
3- Melanin   4- Robert Hooke
5- Right side

1- Which 16-17th century German scientist helped to establish the validity of the Copernican system?
A. Gregor Mendel
B. Johannes Kepler
C. Konrad Lorenz
D. Tycho Brahe

2- Where in the body would you find the conjunctiva?
A. The eye
B. The brain
C. The ear
D. The knee

3- Which of these is a hormone, secreted by the gland in the pancreas?
A. Thyroxine
B. Adrenaline
C. Insulin
D. Sucrase

4- Which of these is NOT a fossil fuel?
A. Fossilized wood
B. Coal
C. Natural gas
D. Petroleum

5- Which of the following is NOT the name of a human tooth?
A. Bicuspid
B. Feline
C. Incisor
D. Molar

Answer

1- Johannes Kepler   2- The eye
3- Insulin   4- Fossilized wood
5- Feline

1- Orange juice is a source of which vitamin?

A. Vitamin A
B. Vitamin B
C. Vitamin C
D. Vitamin D

2- Yellow fever, malaria and dengue are diseases carried by which of these?

A. Cockroaches
B. Pigeons
C. Rats
D. Mosquitoes

3- Red blood cells are needed for people to survive. What is a function of red blood cells?

A. Carry oxygen & carbon dioxide
B. Produce hormones
C. Carry saliva
D. Produce bile

4- If I fractured my scapula, what part of my body is affected the most?

A. Knee
B. Pelvis
C. Toe
D. Shoulder

5- Which planet is nicknamed as the "Red Planet"?

A. Mars
B. Earth
C. Jupiter
D. Venus

Answer

1- Vitamin C   2- Mosquitoes
3- Carry oxygen & carbon dioxide   4- Shoulder
5- Mars

1- Which planet is known as the "Gas giant planet"?

A. Venus
B. Earth
C. Jupiter
D. Mercury

2- Who invented bulb?

A. Albert Einstein
B. Alexander Graham Bell
C. Thomas Edison
D. Nikola Tesla

3- Which animal can store water in its body?

A. Liona
B. Camel
C. Elephant
D. Anaconda

4- How many poles do all magnets have?

A. 1
B. 2
C. 3
D. 4

5- Moon borrows light from which star?

A. The Sun
B. Earth
C. Mars
D. Jupiter

Answer

1- Jupiter   2- Thomas Edison
3- Camel   4- 2
5- The Sun

1- What is the name for the group of organisms which cannot be seen with our naked eye and needs a microscope?

A. Carnivorous

B. Microbes

C. Herbivorous

D. Nocturnal

2- What is the basic unit of life in animals and humans?

A. Organs

B. Brain

C. Cells

D. Skeleton

3- Which of these contains the highest amount of calcium?

A. Sugar

B. Salt

C. Water

D. Milk

4- Which is the softest mineral substance in nature?

A. Bismuth

B. Diamond

C. Rocks

D. Talc

5- Which is the hardest substance in nature?

A. Diamond

B. Emerald

C. Ruby

D. Talc

Answer

1- Microbes   2- Cells

3- Milk   4- Talc

5- Diamond

1- Which camel species has two humps on its back?

A. Arabian camel

B. Dromedary camel

C. Bactrian camel

D. None of these

2- Which condition in animals is characterized by white skin and hair and pink eyes?

A. Albinism

B. Hyperpigmentation

C. Melanism

D. Atrophy

3- Which state would you expect to find water in a glass at room temperature?

A. Gas

B. Solid

C. Liquid

D. None of these

4- How many moons does the planet Mars have?

A. 1

B. 2

C. 3

D. 4

5- Which of these bones is located in our leg?

A. Radius

B. Ulna

C. Tibia

D. Humerus

Answer

1- Bactrian camel   2- Albinism

3- Liquid   4- 2

5- Tibia

Bonus

1: What is the origin of the word algebra?
A. Hindi
B. Latin
C. Arabic
D. Greek

2: Who was the first woman to fly across the Atlantic Ocean alone?
A. Margaret Mitchell
B. Marie Curie
C. Elizabeth Cady Stanton
D. Amelia Earhart

3: In which game is the object to score more runs than your opponent over the course of nine innings?
A. Basketball
B. Football
C. Golf
D. Baseball

4: Who was the Carthaginian leader known for crossing the Italian Alps with elephants?
A. Marco Polo
B. Hannibal
C. Attila the Hun
D. Genghis Khan

5: What is the result of the phenomenon of the earth's plates pushing violently against each other?
A. Earthquake
B. Squall
C. Typhoon
D. Avalanche

Answer

1: Arabic   2: Amelia Earhart
3: Baseball   4: Hannibal
5: Earthquake

1: Which letter is not from the Hebrew alphabet?

A. Omega
B. Yod
C. Tet
D. Gimel

2: What does a philatelist collect?

A. Coins
B. Postcards
C. Stamps
D. Autographs

3: What country does the giant panda inhabit?

A. Canada
B. Australia
C. Kenya
D. China

4: Which animal's name is derived from two Greek words that mean "terrible lizard"?

A. Dinosaur
B. Komodo dragon
C. Chameleon
D. Crocodile

5: What was the name of the Scotland Yard inspector in Sherlock Holmes?

A. Mycroft
B. Hercule Poirot
C. Lestrade
D. Jack Frost

Answer

1: Omega   2: Stamps
3: China   4: Dinosaur
5: Lestrade

1: In which country would you find Utrecht, Arnhem and Maastricht?
A. Belgium
B. France
C. Netherlands
D. Germany

2: What are the two official languages of Finland?
A. Norwegian and French
B. Swedish and Finnish
C. Norwegian and Finnish
D. Danish and German

3: What is the meaning of geology?
A. Study of the earth
B. Study of places
C. Study of space
D. Study of language

4: Where is the world's largest lizard in the world?
A. Gila monster
B. Tasmanian devil
C. Kimono dragon
D. Komodo dragon

5: After elephant, which present-day creature is the heaviest land-dwelling animal?
A. Elephant seal
B. Rhinoceros
C. Giraffe
D. Hippopotamus

Answer

1: Netherlands 2: Swedish and Finnish
3: Study of the earth 4: Komodo dragon
5: Rhinoceros

1: What country was known as Malagasy Republic from 1958-1975?

A. Majorca

B. Madagascar

C. Mali

D. Malta

2: What is the Italian name for Rome?

A. Romi

B. Roam

C. Roma

D. Roman

3: Which of these 1960s events came first?

A. Berlin wall erected

B. John H. Glenn became the first American to orbit the Earth

C. Assassination of President Kennedy

D. George W. Bush is inaugurated as President of the United States

**4: In Rudyard Kipling's 'The Jungle Book',
what was the name of the tiger?**

A. Kaa

B. Shere Khan

C. Bagheera

D. Baloo

5: Which word is not a horse colour?

A. Bay

B. Walnut

C. Roan

D. Chestnut

Answer

**1: Madagascar   2: Roma
3: Berlin wall erected   4: Shere Khan
5: Walnut**

1: Steve Jobs and Steve Wozniak founded what groundbreaking computer company?

A. Apple
B. IBM
C. Oracle
D. Dell

2: What tiny creatures from the diet of the world's largest creature the blue whale?

A. Squid
B. Penguin
C. Seal
D. Krill

3: Athens, Dublin, Moscow and Paris are all European capitals, but they are also cities in a state of the USA. Which state is this?

A. California
B. Arizona
C. Texas
D. New Mexico

4: Which mamba snake tends to be the deadliest?

A. Black mamba
B. Green mamba
C. Red mamba
D. Blue mamba

5: In medieval Britain, the remains of what animal were sometimes placed on the walls of buildings to ward off evil spirits?

A. Snake
B. Fox
C. Cat
D. Dog

Answer

1: Apple   2: Krill
3: Texas   4: Black mamba
5: Cat

Printed in Great Britain
by Amazon

44096949R00059